The Case For CHRIST

FOR KIDS

D0206914

Other books in the Lee Strobel series for kids

The Case for Faith for Kids
The Case for a Creator for Kids
Off My Case for Kids

The Case For
CHRIST
FOR KIDS

Lee Strobel WITH ROB SUGGS

zonder**kidz**

WILLOW
Willow Creek Resources

ZONDERVAN.COM/
AUTHOR**TRACKER**

The children's group of Zondervan

www.zonderkidz.com

The Case for Christ for Kids
Copyright © 2006 by Lee Strobel
Illustrations copyright © 2006 by The Zondervan Corporation

Requests for information should be addressed to:
Grand Rapids, Michigan 49530

Library of Congress Cataloging-in-Publication Data
Strobel, Lee, 1952-
    The case for Christ for kids / by Lee Strobel with Rob Suggs.
      p. cm.
   ISBN-13: 978-0-310-71147-6 (softcover)
   ISBN-10: 0-310-71147-9 (softcover)
     1. Jesus Christ--Person and offices--Juvenile literature.
     2. Apologetics--Juvenile literature. I. Suggs, Rob. II. Title.

BT203.S77 2006
232.9'08--dc22

2005034269

All Scripture quotations, unless otherwise noted, are taken from the Holy Bible: New International Reader's Version®. NIrV®. Copyright © 1995, 1996, 1998 by International Bible Society. Used by permission of Zondervan. All rights reserved.

Scripture quotations marked NCV are taken from the New Century Version. Copyright © 1987, 1988, 1991 by Word Publishing, a division of Thomas Nelson, Inc. Used by permission. All rights reserved.

Scripture quotations marked MSG are from THE MESSAGE. Copyright © by Eugene H. Peterson 1993, 1994, 1995, 1996, 2000, 2001, 2002. Used by permission of NavPress Publishing Group.

Scripture quotations marked NIV are from the Holy Bible, New International Version®. NIV®. Copyright © 1973, 1978, 1984 by International Bible Society. Used by permission of Zondervan. All rights reserved.

All rights reserved. No part of this publication may be reproduced, stored in a retrieval system, or transmitted in any form or by any means — electronic, mechanical, photocopy, recording, or any other — except for brief quotations in printed reviews, without the prior permission of the publisher.

Editor: Kristen Tuinstra
Cover Design: Sarah Jongsma
Interior Art Direction: Sarah Jongsma and Kristen Tuinstra
Interior Design: Sarah Jongsma
Composition: Ruth Bandstra
Illustrations: Dan Brawner

Printed in the United States of America

06 07 08 09 10 • 15 14 13 12 11 10 9 8 7 6

TABLE of Contents

What's Up With That?

Somewhere you took a wrong turn.

This is just the kind of street Mom and Dad warned you to avoid. Run-down apartment buildings line both sides of the road, and the sidewalk is cluttered with garbage.

You need to be home soon, but who can help you? There is one friendly face. She smiles and says her name is Lydia Delgado, and she is eleven. She gives you clear directions back to your neigh-borhood.

You think about Lydia later, and ask your mom if you can go back to thank her. "Only if I go with you," says Mom. So you climb into the car and track down Lydia and her little family. There are only two others: a thirteen-year-old sister, Jenny, and their grandmother, Perfecta. The two sisters have no parents.

What's more, they live in an empty little room with no furniture, no food, no warmth. Lydia and Jenny take turns wearing one sweater as they walk to school. That makes you and Mom sad, but the three who live there seem to be full of smiles.

Your mom has a friend who writes for the newspaper. She tells the story of the Delgado family and says, "Write an article! Your readers need to know about our poor neighbors who need food and shelter."

Christmas Day arrives. You open your shiny new gifts and enjoy a delicious turkey dinner. But afterward, your family decides to pay the Delgados a visit. You have gifts for them and extra turkey and vegetables. So again, you climb into the car.

A Christmas miracle has happened!

Newspaper readers have sent the Delgados boxes and bags of Christmas gifts: warm coats and sweaters for the family, and carpets and chairs for the little apartment. A magnificent Christmas tree illuminates the room, and carols are playing from a little stereo system. The room is drenched in loving gifts from a wealthy city to a poor family.

But that's not the miracle.

Perfecta, Lydia, and Jenny are busy packing many of their gifts back up. As they are writing the names of friends on the boxes, you blurt out, "What are you doing? Why are you giving your gifts away?" You think of your own Christmas—all the new stuff you would never give away.

Perfecta says, "Our neighbors are still in need. We cannot have plenty while they have nothing. This is what Jesus likes us to do." You just stare, your eyes wide. The grandmother continues, "We did nothing to deserve these gifts. But the greatest gift of all is the one we're celebrating today: the gift of Jesus."

You have a lot to think about on the ride home.
When the Delgados were poor, they were happy. When
they were showered with gifts, they seemed exactly
the same. But instead of hoarding their gifts for a rainy
day, their first thought was to share. Why? They said it
had to do with Jesus—what he "likes us" to do. Just as
if he were right here, a living person!

You think about the story your family tells at
Christmas, about the little baby in the manger—two
thousand years ago, right? Exactly *who* was in that
manger? Can he make you as beautiful inside as the
Delgados are?

There was something in the old story about shepherds. An angel told them a baby had been born
nearby, and the shepherds said, "Hey, let's go check it
out." And they did.

You can do the same. Who was in the manger? Is he
real? And how can we be sure?

Go check it out!

PART
one

WHO WAS in the MANGER?

Chapter 1

Who Did This Guy Think He Was?

Did you know there is life on the moon?

Hey, what are you laughing at?

Back in 1835, a newspaper called the *New York Sun* printed an entire series of articles that claimed that life had been discovered on the moon. A famous scientist named Sir John Herschel was said to have rigged up a really effective new telescope. He could look through its lens and see exactly what was happening up on the lunar surface. Supposedly he had spotted buffalo, goats, unicorns, and even winged humanoids who built temples!

Also, it seemed as if the moon would make a terrific vacation site. There were beaches, oceans, and forests up there. You could enjoy them as you took a walk in the earthlight.

Some people got pretty excited. But when someone checked with Sir John Herschel, the whole story fell apart. He said he had no new telescope; he had no idea what was on the moon. But he *did* have a good laugh!

This is what we call a "hoax" today—a story created to attract attention. The crazy story made the *Sun* a very popular paper, even after everyone found out the truth. But it just goes to show you: Don't believe everything you read. When you hear a wild claim, find out the truth for yourself. See if the story holds up.

Actually, that sounds like a pretty good idea for this book. Why not see if the story of Jesus holds up? After all, it's a bigger deal even than goats on the moon. Some people think he was simply a nice guy who taught people to live by the Golden Rule and things like that—just a regular fellow. Others think he never lived at all. Still others believe he was something more than "regular." They say he was the Son of God, and that we should love him and follow him in all that we do.

Golden Rule (gohl-den ROO-el): the virtue of treating others as you would want to be treated.

A lot of differences in those ideas, eh? You need to decide for yourself what you think about Jesus. There are several points for you to look at. First, what did Jesus himself say? Was he crazy or dishonest? And how much evidence is there to support the amazing claims people make about him? Nearly all of Christians' ideas come from the Bible, but how do you know those Bible stories are true? And last there is that matter of coming back from the dead. It's the single most important claim anyone can make about Jesus.

What did the man say about himself?

Most of our information about Jesus comes from one book—the Bible. It's true that historians have found more than one hundred facts about Jesus in other ancient writings. But the Bible is still the most complete source of information about him. So it's important to figure out whether the Bible can be trusted. What if that book is wrong? If somebody disproves the Bible, then that casts a lot of doubt on Jesus. A few pages from now, you take a close look at that question. But for now, you can go to the stories and simply find out what Jesus said.

Historian (his-TOR-ee-en): someone who knows a lot about the past. Historians have found facts about Jesus in other writings like *Josephus* and *Pliny the Younger*.

All of Jesus' stories are found in the New Testament, in four biographies called the "Gospels" (good news books). One of the Gospels is called John. Listen to what it says about Jesus. It calls him "the Word."

> In the beginning, the Word was already there. The Word was with God, and the Word was God. He was with God in the beginning. All things were made through him. Nothing that has been made was made without him … The Word became a human being. He made his home with us. We have seen his glory. It is the glory of the one and only Son.
>
> —John 1:1–3, 14

Stop! Time out! "The Word"? Jesus didn't *say* a word here! This is other people making a big deal about him. If he is something special, we should hear it from his *own* lips. Otherwise it would seem that people made claims about him that he never intended.

Surely he didn't go around calling himself "the Word" or "the One and Only." So we turn over to the longest gospel, the one called Matthew. It has a whole lot of statements from Jesus' mouth, so read on.

Here's a passage that comes right to the point. Jesus asks his friends, "Who do you say I am?" His friend Peter says that Jesus is "the Christ ... the Son of the living God." Again, these people seem eager to make a big deal.

But Jesus does *not* act embarrassed! Far from it. He seems very pleased by Peter's words, and he says, "No mere man showed this to you. My Father in heaven showed it to you" (Matthew 16:15–17). Hmm.

Well, back in John's gospel, they're having still another conversation about this subject. Somebody asks Jesus, "If you are the Christ, tell us plainly." (Yes. *Please!*) Here is how Jesus answers: "I and the Father are one."

It's right there in John 10, verses 24 and 30. If you read a little closer, you find that this was the kind of remark that could get you into hot water—because immediately, the men around Jesus start picking up rocks to throw at him! They said, "'You are only a man. But you claim to be God'" (verse 33).

Jesus called himself ...

The way and the truth and the life	John 14:6
King of the Jews	Luke 23:3
Bread of life	John 6:35
The Messiah	John 4:25–26
The Son of God	John 10:36
The good shepherd	John 10:11
The true vine	John 15:1
The light of the world	John 8:12

I'll believe it when I see it

So the Bible tells us that Jesus said he and the
Father were one. Whatever that means. Are you still
not so sure about all this? It's hard to trust someone
else's word. And guess what? There's a guy just like
you a few pages later! His name was Thomas, and he
was one of Jesus' disciples (his closest friends and
followers). Even there by Jesus' side, he wasn't 100
percent sure that what Jesus was saying was true. At
this point, everybody was claiming Jesus came back
from the dead. Thomas made it clear that he'd agree
as soon as he could see and touch the cuts and scars
on Jesus' hands and feet.

Thomas got his wish. Jesus turned up, gave a show-
and-tell, and Thomas said, "My Lord and my God!"
(John 20:28). Then Jesus said, "You believe because you
see me. Those who believe without seeing me will be
truly happy" (John 20:29 NCV).

We all want to be truly happy. But it's still expecting
a lot for us to believe this man was God. On the other
hand, after looking at the Bible, we have to admit
one thing: Jesus made some mighty big claims about
himself. He wasn't at all shy about calling himself One
with God—or about letting his friends call him such
things.

Well, Jesus talked the talk. So what? Maybe he wasn't telling the truth. He wouldn't be the first guy to stretch the truth a little.

Was Jesus lying about himself?

You've known people who exaggerated their own abilities: "I can beat that video game in one day." Or, "I'm the smartest kid at school." People usually stretch the truth in order to get something they want— respect or attention or things. What about Jesus? What did he have to gain?

You've already seen one answer to that: rocks! In those days, you could be stoned to death just for saying the wrong thing. People had to speak *very* carefully. In Mark's gospel, Jesus was put on trial because of the things he had said. They put him on the spot: "Are you the Christ? Are you the Son of the Blessed One?" (Mark 14:61). And he replied, "I am" (verse 62). Jesus had seen people beaten and crucified. He knew there were many people who wanted to kill him. But that was his story, and he was stuck to it.

Now think about the kid who lies about his video game skills. Would he stick to his story if a whole mob of kids threatened to attack him because of his words? That's what Jesus could get for telling a fib: terrible beatings and then death. He insisted on his claim, and they insisted on killing him.

So what have you learned?

- Jesus did claim to be God.
- That claim got him killed.

CHAPTER 2

WAS JESUS OUT OF HIS MIND?

Lots of insane people walk around claiming to be God. Jesus might have been too crazy to say the right thing and save his own life. How would you know?

You could watch his behavior closely. You would expect an insane person's actions to give him away.

You're not an expert on how crazy people act (no matter how some adults in your life might act). But a professor named Dr. Gary Collins can help. He has spent his career working with those who have mental disorders of all kinds. He offers a list of some of the main signs of insanity. Study his list, then take a good look at whether Jesus acted like a crazy person:

Symptoms of Insanity	Actions of Jesus
Unpredictable emotions—depression or anger at odd times.	Jesus did weep when his friend had died. (John 11) Jesus did become angry when salespeople were cheating the poor. (Luke 19:45–46)
Imagining people are out to get you.	Jesus did believe a friend was out to get him—and he was right. (Matthew 26:14–25, 47–50)
Thinking problems; trouble carrying on logical conversations.	People loved Jesus' teaching. His sermons were orderly and logical. (Matthew 5–7)

Does he sound crazy to you? Wouldn't you cry if one of your friends died? Wouldn't you get angry if you saw someone cheating a poor person? Jesus kept things interesting—no doubt about that. But he never showed any of the classic signs of insanity. He reacted pretty normal in all of these situations.

Here's some evidence that some people thought he was out of his mind:

> *A lot of them were saying, "He's crazy, a maniac—out of his head completely. Why bother listening to him?" But others weren't so sure: "These aren't the words of a crazy man. Can a 'maniac' open blind eyes?"*
>
> —John 10:20–21 MSG

Well, they had a point! Your average crazy person doesn't heal blind people, walk on water, or feed five thousand people from one basket. Many people said they saw Jesus do these things. Crazy people act crazy, they don't perform miracles.

Miracles. They're a pretty important part of all this, aren't they? As we read these Gospels, you can see that Jesus used miracles to show who he really was. They would be pretty good evidence, *if* they were real. After all, you don't often see people walking on water or controlling storms. If the miracles were not real, then that's also evidence. It would mean Jesus was a fake.

These miracles are worth looking into.

Maybe he was a great hypnotist

Perhaps you could hypnotize someone to think you were walking on water or controlling the weather. A good hypnotist could give you water and make you think you were drinking diet cola. Maybe that was how Jesus pulled off that trick where he seemed to change water into wine.

Let's compare Jesus' miracles to hypnotism:

Hypnotism	Miracles
Many people in an audience are resistant to hypnotism.	Jesus performed miracles in huge crowds.
People can usually be hypnotized only when they're willing.	Many of Jesus' enemies saw the miracles. They weren't willing at all!
Hypnotists need words. They can't hypnotize without speaking.	Jesus never spoke to the people who tasted the wine. He never said a word about what he was changing the water into. (John 2:1–11)

So, hypnotism didn't really fit. There were simply too many witnesses. Jesus spoke to large, active crowds. That meant he had to speak up, instead of softly in the way hypnotists talk. He didn't choose certain ideal subjects, but performed miracles everyone could see (including people who didn't want to see miracles at all). Sometimes he even performed miracles that happened miles away! (See John 4:43–54, for instance.) No one can hypnotize someone in the next town.

There was no doubt Jesus was more than just a simple teacher: he was one who calmly and sanely claimed to be God, who did miracles, and died for his claim.

But remember that word Peter called him—"the Christ"? Some think that was just his last name: Mr. Christ. But last names don't make so many people angry, as the use of "Christ" did with Jesus. People seemed as upset about this title as the one of God.

The word *Christ* means "Messiah." Okay, that's helpful. What's *that* one mean?

CASE NOTES

{
_____

_____

_____

_____

_____

_____

_____

_____

_____

_____

_____

_____

_____

_____

_____
}

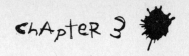

chApteR 3

MessiAh:
DiD Jesus Fit the PictuRe?

The Jews expected a great hero named Messiah to save them one day. The Old Testament had a lot to say about what the Messiah might be like, which gives us a chance to see how Jesus stacked up to that job description. If he

Q4U:

If a great new hero arrived in today's world, what do you think he would be like? What kinds of things would he spend his time on?

fit all the qualifications the Jews had set out for the Messiah long before he was born, that would be even more evidence in Jesus' favor.

Messiah: ancient superhero?

The Jews, Jesus' people, believed that God would send a special person to rescue everyone. Throughout the Old Testament of the Bible, you will find many clues and hints about this hero still to come. The Jews were very eager to meet their Messiah, but they were not sure when to expect him. Jesus claimed he was that special Savior.

You will find references to the Messiah all through the Old Testament, usually in books of the prophets—people who preached about God and sometimes told what God had in store for the future. Finding the Messiah in the Old Testament is like an Easter egg hunt. There's a clue hidden here, another one there, and yet another detail elsewhere.

It takes a good while to make the full "hunt" and get the whole picture. But there were certain details about this coming deliverer that many Jewish people knew. It was known that he would be born in Bethlehem.

He would be descended from David. He would bring a brand new kingdom for Israel, the greatest ever. He would set up his kingdom to last forever.

The box below offers a particularly clear picture of this mysterious Savior.

The Messiah will be faced with these challenges:

Men looked down on him. They didn't accept him. He knew all about sorrow and suffering … But the servant was pierced because we had sinned … He was punished to make us whole again. His wounds have healed us … He took the sins of many people on himself. And he gave his life for those who had done what is wrong.

—Isaiah 53:3, 5, 12

Sound familiar? Yes, it would be hard to come up with a better word picture of the Jesus you know from the New Testament. According to Isaiah, the Messiah would be unpopular with many people and would suffer. Though not doing anything wrong or hurting anyone, he would be "pierced because we had sinned." That means he would accept the punishment (through some sharp weapon) for other people's wrongdoings. He would die among wicked people but be buried among the rich. And because of his wounds, our own hurts would be healed.

From the Gospels, we know that Jesus was indeed unpopular among the religious leaders at the time he was killed. Crowds yelled for his execution. We know he suffered, and that he was pierced with nails and crucified (this punishment was not known in Isaiah's time). He never did anything wrong, never hurt anyone, but died for our wrongs so that we could be healed. It all checks out!

You might think, "That's cool, but it couldn't have been written *before* Jesus lived." As a matter of fact, it was.

Seven hundred years before Jesus, to be exact! It is impossible that it could have been faked, because we know that those precise words of Isaiah (and the other prophets, too) have been there all along, and never changed.

Q4U:

The way you see it, which prediction about the Messiah fits Jesus best? How come?

Five dozen reasons

In all, there are about sixty important predictions about Jesus in the Old Testament. Remember, the prophets were giving details of someone who would not be born for hundreds of years!

Okay, so how about this for an explanation? Jesus knew all those Scriptures. Could it be that he used the predictions as a kind of road map, and went along with following their demands?

The only problem is that there were many prophecy fulfillments he *couldn't* arrange—such as being born in the town of Bethlehem. Micah 5:2 nailed that one. He couldn't arrange to be betrayed for a specific amount of money (Zechariah 11:12–13), or for men to gamble to see who got to keep his clothing (Psalm 22:18).

Well, what about coincidence? Why couldn't there have been several people who fulfilled those prophecies? Jesus might have just been the one who got all the credit. But a science professor named Dr. Peter Stoner says that's highly unlikely. He and six hundred students wanted to find out the likelihood of someone fulfilling so many prophecies. They came up with very reasonable estimates and used a lot of complicated math equations (you don't want to know!) to figure out that the chances of any one person fulfilling just *eight* of the prophecies was one in a hundred million billion.

Coincidence (ko-IN-seh-dents): events that happen at the same time accidentally but seem to have a connection.

Maybe all those figures are wrong. You do the math (or not). Think about this example alone. David wrote, "A group of sinful people has closed in on me. They are all around me like a pack of dogs. They have pierced my hands and feet … They laugh when I suffer. They divide up my clothes among them. They cast lots for what I am wearing" (Psalm 22:16–18). David, who lived long before the Romans and their practice of crucifixion, was writing the thoughts of his own descendant, about one thousand years before that descendant (Jesus) would be born! It seems like too much to be a simple coincidence, doesn't it?

Fitting the big picture

	Prophecies said in the Old Testament	Gospels say in the New Testament
Birth-place	Bethlehem (Micah 5:2)	Bethlehem (Matthew 2:1)
Family	David's line (Jeremiah 23:5–6)	David's line (Matthew 1)
Blood money	30 pieces of silver (Zechariah 11:12–13)	30 pieces of silver (Matthew 26:15)
Gambling for his clothing	Cast lots for clothing (Psalm 22:18)	Cast lots for clothing (Matthew 27:35)

What are the odds?

Jesus knew the importance of all those ancient predictions. He said, "Everything written about me in the Law of Moses, the Prophets and the Psalms must come true" (Luke 24:44). He was certainly aware that he was fulfilling the predictions, but could he have arranged for so many to fit? And if so, why would he do it, knowing his reward would be a cross on a hill?

When Jesus was arrested, he was in a garden praying that there might be some way for him not to face such an awful death. "My soul is very sad. I feel close to death," he said to his friends who were also in the garden. Then he prayed, "My Father, if it is pos–

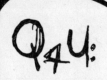

Q44:

So we've looked at what Jesus said and what he did. What did you find most surprising in this section? What did you find most interesting? Why?

sible, take this cup of suffering away from me. But let what you want be done, not what I want" (Matthew 26:38–39). He was not eager to suffer, but would do exactly what his Father wanted him to do.

So what do you think? Do these sound like the words and actions of a crazy person? A faker? What's your take?

If we can trust the Bible, its picture of Jesus is fascinating. If the Gospels are true, there has never been anyone in the world like Jesus. But those are big ifs. The Bible could be a collection of fairy tales. It could be deliberate lies. It could be mistaken.

Couldn't it?

CASE NOTES

PART TWO

DID HIS FRIENDS
TELL THE TRUTH?

ChApteR 4

DoN't Believe eveRYtHiNG YOU ReAD

So you're with your mom, waiting in the checkout line at the grocery store. There are magazines and a couple of colorful newspapers. Wow! Look at the news! It's been a busy day for current events. Aliens have abducted the president of the United States and replaced him with a body double. A wolf-boy has been found roaming the woods of Montana. You think of the story about unicorns and winged humanoids running around on the moon.

With amazing news like this, shouldn't you buy those papers? But Mom says, "Don't believe everything you read."

Parents like to say that because ... well, it's true. Being written down doesn't make it so. And that's exactly where we find ourselves in searching for the truth about Jesus. The Bible's claims about Jesus are *much* more incredible than any claim about a wolf-boy in Montana. The Bible's claims are about miracles, reversing death, and carrying out seven-hundred-year-old prophecies. There's enough stuff there to keep the grocery store papers busy for months.

The claims are written, but are they trustworthy?

Counting the eyeballs

When an event is in question, investigators ask, "How many eyeballs were there?"

In other words, how many people saw the event? To believe something happened, we need witnesses to trust—and the more of them, the better. How many eyeballs can back up Jesus' story? If it was only one fellow who came up with the whole saga, we would all be suspicious.

But the story of Jesus comes from *four* different authors: Matthew, Mark, Luke, and John. We call them the Gospels, which is a word meaning *good news.* But was it news at all, or was it pretending to be news? You have to study them closely to decide.

John, for example, was a disciple. His eyeballs were on the scene, and he is eager for us to understand that. He says he is telling us about things "which we have heard, which we have seen with our eyes, which we have looked at and our hands have touched" (1 John 1:1 NIV).

What they wrote and why

Matthew	Disciple of Jesus. Wrote to show Jewish readers how Jesus fulfilled the old prophecies.
Mark	Close friend of the disciple Peter. First of the four to write a gospel. Eager to tell the simple facts.
Luke	A doctor who was a companion of Paul, an eyewitness of the resur-rected Jesus. Luke talked to Mary and many others, making a full and careful investigation of what happened.
John	Disciple who wanted to share the facts that showed Jesus was the Son of God.

Luke is a first-rate reporter, offering plenty of checkable details. Listen to what he says: "I myself have carefully looked into everything from the beginning. So it seemed good also to me to write down an orderly report of exactly what happened" (Luke 1:3). Then there's Mark, who got much of his account from Peter, a particularly close friend of Jesus.

By the way, Peter's story is not just in Mark—it's also in his own writings. He says, "We didn't make up stories when we told you about it. With our own eyes we saw him in all his majesty" (2 Peter 1:16).

Are you surprised that the gospel writers *expected* people to have questions about their amazing stories? They were careful to show that their accounts came from eyewitnesses. And everybody knows that in a court of law—or in trying to figure out what happened long ago—eyewitness accounts are very persuasive.

When you hear different stories, how do you decide who is telling the truth? What kinds of things do you consider?

What about their differences?

Here's another question. Do the gospel writers agree on all the details? Well, they do provide different perspectives. So isn't that a big problem? If these four couldn't get their stories straight, what are you supposed to think?

> Perspective (per-SPEK-tiv): someone's point of view of a subject or an event. For example, his *perspective* of exactly what happened in a big football play is based on the location of his seat in the stadium.

It happens all the time. Imagine four people see an automobile accident on Main Street. There are going to be little differences in their stories of what they saw happen. Who is right? Or are all of them wrong? (See box.)

Here's something surprising about testimony differences. History experts say that little variations make a story more believable! Why? Because that's life. We all see things from different positions. People tend to be clear about the main thing that they see—for instance, which car rammed into the other one. But they also miss little things (for instance, what color shirts the drivers were wearing). History books are filled with different perspectives among people who were there

for wars and other great events. But when it comes to who won the battle and what the main events were, they are on the same page.

This is certainly the case with the four Gospels. On every key point, they agree. On the little things, they sometimes offer different perspectives and details.

Whose side of the story?

Someone reports a fight in the school cafeteria. Four kids are questioned about the incident — but their stories don't quite match!

Does this mean:

a. The fight never happened?

b. There's one honest kid and three liars?

c. All are truthful but had different perspectives?

If you think about it, most of the time the answer is c. Observers emphasize different details. The little variations make them more believable, not less so.

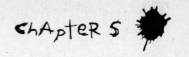

ChApteR 5

It's A coNspiRAcy!

Let's try another one. Maybe Matthew, Mark, Luke, and John were four guys who entered into a conspiracy. Maybe they really wanted their new church to be successful, so they agreed to make up a story and stick to it. Maybe it was all a big prank. Could that explain the stories of Jesus?

> Conspiracy (kun-SPEER-ehsy): an agreement between people who are trying to cover up that they did something wrong or illegal.

To repeat our last point, if they had made up the story, their accounts would have been suspiciously consistent. But there's a larger point. People tend to lie when there is something to be gained. Your classmate might claim her father is a millionaire, for instance. Rewards? Friends would be impressed. They would invite her to more parties. (The lie is unlikely to succeed for very long, of course.)

Consistent (kuhn-SIS-tent): when two or more sides of the story are exactly the same.

How about Matthew, Mark, Luke, and John? Was a more successful church their reward? History clearly tells us that early Christians were rewarded with … *death*. Christianity wasn't too popular with public leaders for a few centuries. Most of the disciples were killed by people who were angry about these stories of a dead man who rose again. So if the gospel writers were lying, they did so at the strong risk of death. Do you think they would lie under those conditions?

Another reason lying would be unlikely is the painful account of Jesus. The gospel writers told how people jeered at him and wanted him to die. They told the manner of his death. Crucifixion was considered a mark of shame in those days. Paul wrote, "But we preach about Christ and his death on the cross. That is very hard for Jews to accept. And everyone else thinks it's foolish" (1 Corinthians 1:23). Why make up a story that people won't accept or will think is foolish?

Fact-checkers

Magazines hire "fact-checkers." These are people who carefully check all the facts and make sure mistakes don't slip into the news story.

The four Gospels were surrounded by fact-checkers, so how could they lie? People were still alive who could remember seeing Jesus in person. If these amazing stories had been lies, wouldn't there have been many people coming forward to set the record straight?

But shortly after Jesus was killed, Peter talked to a large crowd about "miracles, wonders and signs among you through Jesus. You yourselves know this." He went on to say, "God has raised this same Jesus back to life. We are all witnesses of this" (Acts 2:22, 32).

That's about the same as you saying, "I transformed into a giant eggplant last Tuesday in the school cafeteria, and you saw it yourself." You couldn't get away with saying something like that *unless* it really happened. The only people likely to believe a wild story are those who saw it and know it's true. And Paul wrote about Jesus to such people.

As a matter of fact, we are told that when Peter talked to that crowd, three thousand people took his advice and became followers of Christ. Jesus was

mighty popular for a "dead" man! You can read the whole story in Acts 2. It's a wild one!

> *What Paul said about it...*
>
> *"I passed on to you ... Christ died for our sins, just as Scripture said he would. He was buried. He was raised from the dead on the third day. ... He appeared to Peter. Then he appeared to the Twelve. After that, he appeared to more than 500 believers at the same time. Most of them are still living."*
>
> *−1 Corinthians 15:3−6*

Replay

You've a learned a lot so far. The Gospels cannot be easily dismissed as made-up stories or lies. There is

Would thousands of people have become Christians if the disciples were making up wild stories?

too much good evidence and common sense on the other side of the question. We also know that the story of Jesus has stood the test of time. For two thousand years, no one has been successful in disproving it. That's a pretty strong record.

The story is so strong because it was told by eye-witnesses who were willing to die for their story. Jesus didn't seem to be a liar, act like a crazy person, or try to hypnotize people. Neither did the people who followed him. Smart people believed in him.

The question is, so what? If a man performed miracles twenty centuries ago, why should that be a big deal today? Imagine someone discovering tomor-row that dinosaurs still walk the earth in a remote corner of South America. It would be a big story, there would be TV reports, but what happens after the surprise wears off? Wouldn't we all just go back to what we were doing before they found the big reptiles?

If dinosaurs still walked in South America, wouldn't it be cool to see them? Like a dino zoo!

The difference is that many people *still* follow Jesus. They seem to find that following Jesus makes their lives better. It makes them happier even when times are rough, as with the Delgados. It gives them answers for their questions about how to live. Following Jesus gives them a friendship like no other.

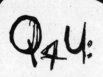

The way you see it, what does believing in Jesus have to do with the way you live and treat others? How come?

If Jesus could do miracles then, and if death is no problem for him—can he do miracles now? The only thing to do is keep on the trail. It's time to investigate the biggest question of all: whether a person can come back from the dead.

CASE NOTES

{

_____

_____

_____

_____

_____

_____

_____

_____

_____

_____

_____

_____

}

PART THREE

CAN A DEAD MAN COME BACK?

coming BACK FROM the DeAD?

Hey, it happens every day.

At least, it happens on television. For example, think about the story *Pinocchio*. He comes back to life as a real boy. The Beast in *Beauty and the Beast*, killed in a fight—comes back to life as a handsome prince. *Snow White, Sleeping Beauty*—dead one minute, off to a wedding the next. In all kinds of stories, there's nothing more exciting and dramatic than a *resurrection*.

> Resurrection (rez-er-ECK-shun): when someone comes back to life after dying.

But that's kid stuff, right? Fairy tale material. Or it's even *more* unbelievable, like in a scary movie. A mummy that comes to life and chases people around. Resurrection never happens in the real world. Or does it?

Well, this is THE big question when we talk about Jesus. Christians insist that Jesus did exactly that. They say that he died, was buried, then rose after three days in his tomb. They say that he offered the same power over death to his followers. That's what the good news is all about: not having to be afraid of death.

If you think about it, even his greatest miracles would have been forgotten otherwise.

Not quite dead

If you heard that a man fell down dead, then got up and walked away, what would be your first thought?

The Bible says Jesus walked on water and stopped a big storm. Why isn't that a bigger deal than reviving after death, in your opinion? What makes resurrection so special?

You might blurt out, "He wasn't really dead! He was just knocked out."

There are a few of these "after death" stories from time to time. In the hospital, patients can be pronounced dead, only to revive a moment or two later. We understand, of course, that these people did not *really* die. It just seemed that way to the doctors.

That's what many people have suggested about Jesus. It seems more believable than really coming back from the dead, doesn't it? Jesus died on a Roman cross. But maybe in this one case, the guys didn't get the job done. Maybe they pulled him down a little early, laid him in the cave, and went home to dinner. Later on, Jesus opened his eyes, feeling a little weak and sore. When he returned to his friends, they just assumed it was a miracle—that he had really come back from the dead. Then they could say, "Hey, he really is the Messiah after all!"

Or say … maybe it was no accident at all, but one more part of Jesus' make-the-prophecies-happen plan. Maybe Jesus took a special knock-out drug that would make him seem dead for a couple of days. He faked his own death, knowing all along that coming back would make him a big sensation.

Let's take a closer look at these not-quite-dead theories.

Did he fake the whole thing?

The fake-death crowd offers three items of evidence to support their view:

Mark 15:36 says that on the cross, Jesus was offered some drink on a sponge. A drug?

Mark 15:44 says Pilate was surprised by Jesus' quick death. Was he buried too quickly?

Jesus walked and talked later. Could it be he never died at all?

What are some words that describe the emotions you might have felt if you had been Jesus' friend, and seen him being whipped?

But now let's look at the other side. Those two verses from Mark are interesting—but a good investigator must consider *all* the evidence.

Blood, sweat, and tears. Remember when Jesus went to pray in the garden? He wept and prayed, and "his sweat was like drops of blood" (Luke 22:44). That's a pretty strange diagnosis from a doctor, wouldn't you think? When was the last time you had bloody sweat?

Turns out Luke was a good doctor after all. Today we know about a rare condition (hematidrosis) that matches Luke's description. And what causes this bloody sweat? Grief and anxiety. Blood goes right into the sweat glands.

Stripped and whipped. Jesus received a severe beating at the hands of the Roman guards. They would have removed his clothing and used a whip of braided leather. So terrible was this torture that some victims never made it to the cross.

Why is this important? It tells us that Jesus would have been in a very serious medical condition before he even made it up to the cross. Hold that thought for a moment.

Rated V for violent

The truth about crucifixion is shocking, isn't it? You can see just how painful and terrible it was for Jesus. Yet he stayed in Jerusalem, knowing these things would happen to him! Why would he do that? Christians believe he was willing to accept a painful death so that God would forgive the sins (or wrongs) of all those who love Jesus and understand what he did for them. In other words, he was volunteering for the punishment the rest of us would earn for all our sins throughout our lives. How does that make you feel about Jesus?

CASE NOTES

chapter 7

A Body on the Cross

Most of us have seen pictures of Jesus on a cross, but those images usually don't tell the whole story. The cross remains one of the cruelest torture methods ever invented. It was slow, painful, and terrible in every way.

First there were the thick spikes (not thin little nails). When hammered through the wrist, they would have damaged the large nerve that enters the hand. The cross would then be thrust into the earth before the ankles received the same treatment.

The weight of the victim's body, pulling against the nails, would have extended his arms by about six inches, according to scientists.

Death came from lack of breathing. Hanging in this position, a victim would have to push up with his feet to breathe. After pushing up too much, the victim would be very tired. The heart would beat irregularly, and death would come through heart failure. According to what the Gospels say, they fit all the facts that modern doctors say about this kind of death.

Found in a cave

Critics once claimed that crucifixion as described in the Gospels was impossible. They said that nails or even spikes would not support the weight of a body. But in 1968, in a cave near Jerusalem, the remains of a crucified body were found. The male was in his twenties, and his wounds matched the descriptions of Jesus' wounds.

Put it all together

Now, think about what you learned about the whipping that would have left Jesus terribly injured. Think about the nerves to the hands being destroyed, as well as the difficulty in breathing. If Jesus somehow survived all of this by being taken from the cross a little early—what kind of shape do you think he would have been in three days later?

> **More about crucifixion**
>
> Many ancient cultures used crucifixion as a way to execute people, but the Romans did so for nearly one thousand years. On one occasion, after stopping a slave revolt led by a man named Spartacus, the Romans crucified six thousand rebels at one time.

He wouldn't have appeared fit and healthy as the Gospels tell us he appeared. Instead, he would have looked gruesome! The disciples would have called a doctor, not launched a worldwide movement based on the wonderful claim that they would someday overcome death as Jesus did.

To believe Jesus didn't die on the cross, you must choose certain facts in the gospel and ignore others—and that's not a very effective way to come to the most accurate conclusion.

Was the tomb really empty?

Being realistic, we must agree that Jesus could not have survived the execution described in his four biographies. So the whole question comes down to his burial place, doesn't it? Either that tomb held the body of a dead Jewish teacher or it didn't.

So ... was the tomb really empty? Remember, people were saying, "Jesus is alive! He must be the Son of God!" And what would you have expected Jesus' enemies to say? If the dead body had still been there, they could have brought it out and quickly and easily dried up all the excitement. But in Matthew 28:13, the leaders only said, "They stole his body while we were sleeping." In other words, they admitted it was missing.

So was the body stolen?

Maybe the religious leaders were right. Many skeptical people have tried to claim that Jesus' followers stole the body then claimed a resurrection. But let's think about what this would have required.

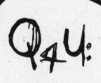

Why do you think the leaders of Jesus' time were so intent on discouraging Jesus' followers? Why do you think some people today might feel the same way?

Jesus was not buried in a hole in the ground, but a cave—actually a tiny room cut out of rock. A large, disk-shaped rock blocked the one small entrance. You could easily roll the rock downhill into place, but it would take many strong men to roll it back up. So a great deal of organized effort was required.

Also, the tomb was guarded. Matthew 27:63–66 tells us that Jesus' enemies were worried that the body would be stolen to fulfill Jesus' prediction that he would rise after three days. "'Take some guards with you,' Pilate answered. 'Go. Make the tomb as secure as you can.'" So they went and made the tomb secure. They put a seal on the stone and placed some guards on duty" (verses 65–66).

So highly trained Roman guards stood by the tomb. Do you think it would have been easy for a few of Jesus' friends to get by them and break in? Remember they would have run a very high risk of being beaten and crucified.

Would the Romans have stolen the body? They had no reason to do so.

Would the religious leaders have stolen the body? As we have seen, they took measures to keep the body from being stolen.

Q44:

What conclusion do you draw about whether Jesus really died? What conclusion do you draw about what happened to his body?

What about the disciples?

There is one other piece to the resurrection puzzle. Why would the disciples change so much in their courage and hope?

When Jesus was arrested, they went into hiding. They were afraid they would be arrested, too. Even when they heard the first reports that Jesus was not in his tomb, they were reluctant to believe. "But the apostles did not believe the women. Their words didn't make any sense to them" (Luke 24:11). Like most of the world, they considered the idea of rising from the dead to be ridiculous.

But something happened. Within a few years, the same disciples were leading a movement that spread all across the Roman Empire—even though many believers were punished or killed for joining it. Of the eleven remaining

disciples (Judas, the betrayer, was dead), Christian history records that ten were executed for their faith. Their belief gave them that much courage.

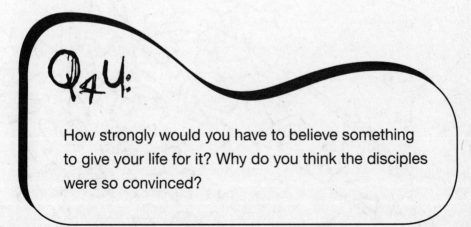

Q4U:

How strongly would you have to believe something to give your life for it? Why do you think the disciples were so convinced?

chapter 8

The Further Adventures of Jesus

Elvis Presley was a rock star. During the 1950s, he was the most popular singer in America. And his fans continued to buy each of his records and see each of his movies until he died in 1977.

Many of them were so devoted to Elvis they just couldn't believe that he was dead. Over the years, "Elvis sightings" have been reported in grocery store tabloids (the kind of newspapers that have alien and wolf-boy stories). There have been jokes and even movies about finding Elvis as alive as ever. People have fun imagining, but they don't really believe he is alive. Why?

Simply because there isn't any good evidence that he isn't still in his grave.

What about Jesus? There were "Jesus sightings," but couldn't they have been like the wolf-boy tales of their time? Couldn't they have been legends and tall tales?

The Gospels give us several stories of public appearances made by Jesus after his burial. Our job is to decide whether those stories are believable.

How about five hundred eyewitnesses?

The most dramatic report of a Jesus sighting is found in a letter by Paul the Apostle. In 1 Corinthians 15:3–6, Paul lists the evidence for his readers. He says that Jesus died, was buried, and rose after three days, just as the prophecies had said. Paul affirmed that Jesus "appeared to Peter. Then he appeared to the Twelve. After that, he appeared to more than 500 believers at the same time. Most of them are still living" (verses 5–6).

In other words, the world was still filled with people who had seen and spoken with a resurrected Jesus! Paul wrote this letter knowing that many would pass it around. Do you think he would have made such a statement if it could be easily disproved? He basically said, "Plenty of folks saw and spoke to Jesus. Ask them yourself!"

Urban legend?

Have you heard of urban legends? They're stories that are passed around and believed, but aren't true. There is an urban legend that the sewers of New York City have crocodiles! That one has been disproved many times. Couldn't the Jesus sightings be urban legends of their time?

The main problem with this theory is that there wasn't enough time for a legend to grow. Scholars and historians tell us that legends (such as King Arthur or Robin Hood) take hundreds of years to develop. They also begin small and grow larger. But Paul wrote his account about five hundred eyewitnesses before the Gospels were written. As he said, he was writing within the lifetime of eye-witnesses. The shocking claim of a resurrection would quickly be disproved—unless it was true.

Also, myths and urban legends never "name names." You can never find someone who actually witnessed the event that is claimed. But Paul and the gospel writers offered names, places, and details for Jesus' appearances. And remember, Luke was a doctor and a serious historian who was committed to investigation and truth.

Hallucinations?

Some people have suggested that the disciples were so emotionally overcome that they began "seeing things." They missed Jesus so deeply that they imagined him back with them.

Hallucinations (huh-LOO-sen-AY-shuns): seeing people or things that aren't really there.

But experts on hallucinations insist that they are not a group activity. People have individual hallucinations—not in groups of eleven or of five hundred. And once again, wouldn't they have gone to the grave and checked? Wouldn't an unoccupied tomb have cured their hallucinations?

Finally, remember that these disciples—and many early Christians—were willing to die for this idea. Would they have died for a hallucination or something that was not totally convincing?

Even more adventures of Jesus

There is only one more avenue of evidence—that of Jesus continuing to walk and talk with believers.

Evidence from the past is very important. But what about evidence that is still fresh? Perhaps the greatest reason of all for the faith of hundreds of millions of Christians around the world is that they know Jesus as a friend, right now. There is a character in American legends named Paul Bunyan. It would be easy to convince you that he never actually lived (he didn't). But if you have a good friend who goes to school with you and talks to you on the phone, it would be *very* difficult to convince you that he didn't exist!

That's the way many people are with Jesus. They believe he once lived, once died, once rose again, and still lives today. They know it because they talk to him in prayer every day. They know it because they can feel his presence with them as they go about their daily lives. And they know it because he has brought many good changes to their lives.

The Delgados, from way back at the beginning of this book, were people like that. They lived the way they knew Jesus wanted them to live, and it made them happier in every way. It caused good things and tough things in life to make sense. And they knew that when they had a problem or a challenge of any kind, Jesus would be there to love and help them. Through his teachings in the Bible, Jesus offers wonderful advice for every problem to people like the Delgados.

They also knew that life's greatest fear—death—can be managed because Jesus rose from the dead two thousand years ago. The evidence is convincing: Jesus was telling the truth when he said that whoever believed in him would not die but have eternal life. (See John 3:16.)

In other words, the story of Jesus is not a fairy tale. But it does have one thing in common with those stories: it has a happy ending. Jesus has promised that no matter what you face, there will be a happy ending for all of his friends. And when you know that, you have a whole new attitude about life—an attitude of excitement and hope.

What now?

So where do you go from here?

Imagine you're just the way you were at the beginning of the book. You were taking a walk when you became lost and found the Delgados. But this time you have found someone else.

You ask him, "Where to now?"

He smiles and puts a hand around your shoulder like a good friend. As he does so, you see the scar on his wrist left by a nail long ago. Your friend says, "Where do you want to go?"

You reply, "Well, I thought I was lost ..."

And your friend says, "That's one of the good things! There are many roads to take. Some lead home, and some lead to new adventures. But whichever road you take, I will go with you. I will always be available to encourage you and care for you. That's what friends do. And in the end, you will find that all roads lead to the same place. You and I will go to a wonderful home I have prepared for you. But that's in the future. Until then, you have adventures to experience and wisdom to learn. Until then, you have one day after another, each one offering its own gift and its own surprise. Come on—walk with me."

As they say, the adventure of a lifetime begins with one step. Which step will you take today?

Check out this
excerpt from
The Case for
Faith for Kids!

The Case for FAITH
FOR KIDS

Lee Strobel with Rob Suggs

zonderkidz

Any Questions?

Hey, do you like questions?

Questions are cool. They come in several flavors. Of course, there are the boring questions:

Who was the thirteenth president of the United States?

What is the state bird of Montana?

Then there are those corny questions called riddles:

Why did the chicken cross the playground?

Answer: To get to the other *slide*.

There are also the head–scratching, noggin–tickling questions:

Why do people drive on a parkway but park on a driveway?

Why does "after dark" occur after light?

Why are whales still chubby after all that swimming?

Why don't sheep shrink in the rain?

Why do cameras have round lenses but take square pictures?

Why does night fall but day break?

Why is one of the hottest dishes called "chili"?

Why are many people afraid of heights, but no one is afraid of widths?

Those questions probably have answers, but who cares? They're more interesting the way they are, don't you think?

Then there are questions that *do* have answers. For example, do you ever stand on the beach and wonder how the moon way up *there* causes all those waves way down *here*? Or how long it would take to travel to another galaxy?

You could get those answers without much problem. That's why there's science. The kind of science called *physics* would tell you about the moon and tides. *Astron-omy* would tell you about how long to plan for an intergalactic vacation.

Big-league questions

Then there are those questions that everyone won-ders about at some time or another:

How did this world get here?

Is there a God?

Which religion is true?

In case you're interested, a book called *The Case for a Creator* worked on the God question. Another one called *The Case for Christ* covered questions about Jesus, such as: Was he really the Son of God? Could he really have risen from the dead?

This book is filled with big-league questions about believing in God and following Christ. Even a lot of Christians wonder about these noggin-nibblers:

If God is good, why does he let bad things happen in the world?

Do miracles happen or does science prove they are impossible?

Is Jesus the only way to get into heaven? What about other religions?

If I have questions or doubts, does that mean I'm not a Christian?

Herbivorous: an animal that only eats plants. They're vegetarians — no burgers for them!

Why ask in the first place?

Those are some brain-drainers, and that's a ... well, a no-brainer. People ask these questions all the time, and why shouldn't they? The answers are very important. It's only natural that folks would wonder.

One more question: Should people who already believe in God ask for answers? If they wonder, for instance, whether God is really fair, does that mean they don't trust God enough? Should they just ignore the tough stuff and go on believing in God?

No, because questions are too pesky to let us do that. They have a way of hanging around like stray cats in your neighborhood. If you pay even a little bit of attention to a stray, he'll keep showing up at your door. If you pay a little attention to an important question, it'll keep showing up in your mind.

Here's an example. *Don't think of a green-striped hippo.* Go ahead—try not to think of a massive, blubbery, herbivorous, four-toed aquatic artiodactyl mammal with lime green racing stripes. Here is some blank space for you to spend *not thinking* about that.

See? Before, it was easy not to think of one. But once you read those words, *green-striped hippo*, there you go. The more you try not to think of one, the more he makes himself at home inside your brain.

Artiodactyl: hoofed mammals with an even number of toes. Animals like cows, deer, sheep, camels, goats, and hippopotamuses. (Even green-striped hippos!)

The Case for Faith
For Kids

Based on *The Case for Faith*, this inspirational edition for kids ages eight to twelve develops the case for having faith in God. Using words kids understand, coupled with humor, sidebars, and more, *The Case for Faith for Kids* helps kids gain an understanding of what having faith really means.

SOFTCOVER 0-310-71146-0

Available at your local bookstore!

zonder**kidz**

WILLOW
Willow Creek Resources

THe CASE FOR A CREATOR
FOR KIDS

Lee Strobel's award-winning book analyzed scientific evidence to build a convincing case that the universe was designed by God. Now revised for kids, with fun extras and easy-to-understand explanations of scientific theory, *The Case for a Creator for Kids* demystifies the creation of the universe in a way that should settle questions once and for all.

SOFTCOVER 0-310-71148-7

Available at your local bookstore!

zonder**kidz**

WILLOW
Willow Creek Resources

Off My Case for Kids

A great companion book or for use all by itself, *Off My Case for Kids* presents twelve real-life scenarios to help kids visualize how they might defend their faith when challenged by unbelievers. Also suggests nonconfrontational ways to handle it, as well as Scripture memory and journaling pages to help put thoughts in their own words.

SOFTCOVER 0-310-71199-1

Available at your local bookstore!

zonder**kidz**   **WILLOW**
Willow Creek Resources

ZONDERVAN.COM/
AUTHOR**TRACKER**

We want to hear from you. Please send your comments about this this book to us in care of zreview@zondervan.com. Thank you.

Grand Rapids, MI 49530
www.zonderkidz.com